for Julie

Contents

Dear Alice

NARRATIVES OF MADNESS

TOM POW

SALT

LONDON

PUBLISHED BY SALT PUBLISHING
Fourth Floor, 2 Tavistock Place, Bloomsbury, London WC1H 9RA United Kingdom

© Tom Pow, 2008, 2009

Salt Publishing 2008, 2009

Printed in Great Britain by the MPG Books Group, Bodmin and King's Lynn

Typeset in Swift 9.5 / 13

ISBN 978 1 84471 416 2 hardback
ISBN 978 1 84471 740 8 paperback

1 3 5 7 9 8 6 4 2

Dear Alice

TOM POW has won three Scottish Arts Council Book Awards for his poetry and one for his children's writing. He has also written a travel book and written radio dramas. From 2001 to 2003 he was the first writer in residence at the Edinburgh International Book Festival and in 2005 was Poet in Residence at StAnza, Scotland's Poetry Festival. He has taught in Edinburgh, London, Madrid and Dumfries. He teaches at Glasgow University, Crichton Campus in Dumfries, where he is a Senior Lecturer in creative writing and storytelling. In 2007, he received a Creative Scotland Award.

Also by Tom Pow

POETRY

Transfusion with illustrations by Hugh Bryden (Shoestring Press, 2007)

Sparks! with Diana Hendry (Mariscat, 2005)

Landscapes and Legacies (inyx, 2003)

Landscapes with linocuts by Hugh Bryden (Cacafuego Press, 1999)

Red Letter Day (Bloodaxe Books, 1996)

The Moth Trap with wood engravings by Jonathan Gibbs (Canongate, 1990)

Rough Seas with wood engravings by Jonathan Gibbs (Canongate, 1987)

WRITING FOR CHILDREN

Captives (Corgi, 2006)

The Pack (Red Fox, 2004)

Tell Me One Thing, Dad with illustrations by Ian Andrew (Walker Books, 2004)

Scabbit Isle (Corgi, 2003)

Who is the World For? with illustrations by Robert Ingpen (Walker Books, 2000)

Callum's Big Day with illustrations by Mairi Hedderwick (inyx, 2000)

TRAVEL

In the Palace of Serpents: An Experience of Peru (Canongate, 1992)

AS EDITOR

Shouting it Out: Stories from Contemporary Scotland (Hodder & Stoughton, 1995)

Acknowledgements

In 2000, I began to work for Glasgow University at the Crichton Campus in Dumfries, the site of one of the great nineteenth century asylums. The poems in *Dear Alice—Narratives of Madness* are rooted in this experience. Although I have made use of documented evidence for many of the poems, others are drawn from a daily experience of working within the Crichton grounds. Whatever their source, they are all works of the imagination. I am indebted to Morag Williams, Archivist to NHS Dumfries and Galloway based on the Crichton site, for her enthusiasm and her deep knowledge of the Crichton. She guided me towards sources that were of immeasurable value.

I am grateful to the Scottish Arts Council for a writer's bursary and to the University of Glasgow for the time without commitments in which to work on *Dear Alice—Narratives of Madness*.

Some of these poems have appeared in the following: *New Writing 13* (Picador), *Poetry Scotland*, *Southlight*, *The Scottish Poetry Library Newsletter*, *Both Sides of Hadrian's Wall*, *60/60* (Daemon), *Markings*, the on-line magazine *Mad Hatter's Review* and the SPL website. The title poem, 'Dear Alice' was previously published in *Sparks!* (Mariscat, 2005—with Diana Hendry). 'Inmates', after an artwork by Jan Hogarth in the Crichton grounds, was first published as a postcard. I am grateful to the editors and collaborators involved in all these earlier appearances. 'Questions of Judgement' was the result of a commission from composer, Ali Burns. I am especially grateful to her for alerting me to the potential of what was all around me.

TOM POW
DUMFRIES, AUGUST 2007

Everything possible to be believ'd
is an image of truth.

from *Proverbs of Hell* by WILLIAM BLAKE

Prelude

It's one of those mornings
when it's a blessing to be
up and about. The chestnuts
wear the early light with grace,
the grass is silver with dew.

A young, tawny cat pads
over the path before him—
in its mouth, the early
morning sparrow, its beak still
soundlessly praising the day.

Inauguration

He casts an eye round the brightly painted room—
the perfect pot plants, the prints on the walls,
the audience at their tables
down to their last sips of wine.

"Let us remember," he begins, "what's most remarkable
about the very room we're in tonight—
only last year it was home
to the criminally insane.

"And we're delighted," he continues,
"that some of them are able to join us now."

They shuffle in—the criminally insane.
One carries a sparrow jammed in his mouth;
one swishes a dead chicken through a spill
of blood red wine. The crowd

eases back, not wishing
to cause offence, demonstrating more
than a clear willingness to share the space
with its former inmates.

We are a *Liberal* Arts College, after all.

But the criminally insane have a spokesperson too,
a small man with electrified hair,
who wishes us to know what's most
remarkable about this space

is how many of the dead
once moved here. "So please, with me,
welcome back the dead." And the dead
mooch in, lifting their heavy lids to the light.

They look around, approvingly it's clear,
at the decor, at us and at the fidgeting
criminally insane. "Remarkable . . .

"Remarkable . . ." the chairman repeats
as a sound of thunder fills the air
and the foundations
start to shake.

Song for M

it began with a hen
which fell in a pond

and a girl named M
who plunged in the pond
to save the hen

her blood bloomed
in the water

2.

once her blood
bloomed in the water
M caught a cold

she had no stopper

the hen flapped
its useless wings

and M plunged
            headlong
into madness

3.

what plunged **M**
         headlong
into a cold hen

her blood had
bloomed in the water

but **M** saved
her madness then

far from the pond
she outlived that hen
the end

Nebuchadnezzar in the Arboretum by Moonlight

Nothing but madness till now, the hard earth
callusing my hands, the snow and the rain
seeping through cracked skin. Though it was birth
of a kind at first to leave far behind
that other madness—my name on each brick
of the city, each flower willed into place
by me—and to fall on all fours, to lick
dirt, let it matt with the hair of my face.

But let those who can still read, read the signs:
cherry trees stand amazed in their own moons
of blossom, while I root through the rich wines
of the earth. I'll excavate a new song
to last till my empire falls. Let all fall—
apart from these trees and one well-lit hall.

From Foucault: Two Tales and a Bedlam Ballad

1. APPETITE

A man, believing himself to be dead,
stopped eating. The world became a plaything

of shadows. Spectres haunted him daily.
But Death, he discovered, was thin gruel—

there was no nourishment to be found there.
In for the long haul, he took to his bed.

Dying, however, remained active long after
he'd thought it disarmed. Nothing for it

but to soldier on till the cupboard
of memory was bare. A few of his friends

disguised themselves. They whitened
their faces then shrouded their forms

in loose fitting black gowns. They entered
his room, set up a table before him

and brought to it a spread of bread, meat,
cheese, chocolate and wine. They ate and drank

then replenished the feast. He stared at them
from out of the hollows of his fading eyes.

But why they asked him did he stay in bed?
Didn't he realise dead people eat as much

as the living ever did? They helped him
up and they ate together through the night.

As dawn broke, they rejoiced at his rebirth—
the colour that flooded his cheeks, the energy

with which he cracked a chicken wing apart.
Yet they wondered, as they rose from the table,

how he'd lit the hunger in their bellies,
that drew them back to these splintered bones.

2. THE WISE FARMER

It was said, between Tinwald
and Torthorwald, lived a farmer
who could cure the mad. A Hercules
of a man, he yoked two to the plough—

and if one shrugged at the traces
he larded the stick across his back.
They were kept naked
and dark as the earth itself

and, as the plough thrust in—
cleaving to one side clods,
roots and rocks—the tendons
of their necks were guyed like ropes,

the clenched muscles of their flanks
clear as if they'd been flayed.
In the cloudbursts of spring
blindly they lifted their faces

and the rain washed them
like stones. They were as nothing
from where the rains came—as peewits
in the vast open rigs of sky.

Madness, the farmer instructed
his neighbours, is the bestial
raised in man. The trick's to restore
to man the animal that rages

in his heart. With Reason beaten,
docility's assured. Below Torthorwald,
come evening, the Lochar Moss
is groomed with gold. He unshackles

his pair and leads them to the byre.
After feeding, they crouch down
together in their stall. They tend
the raw burns on their shoulders,

the welts across their backs. Neighbours
claim they hear them howl, insist their door
is firmly snecked. Still the wise farmer
has his champions and it's said,

if you travel between Tinwald
and Torthorwald, it's hard to tell
which half of the men might be beasts —
or which of the beasts be men.

3. GLASS

Because I'm made of glass,
I must beware I break.
Because I'm made of fire,
I can't give back what I take.

Because I'm made of water,
I must cup every drop.
Because I'm made of iron,
I must cradle other crops.

Because I'm made of ice,
I must keep out the sun.
Because I'm made of pain,
I keep away from guns.

Because I'm made of love,
I find I'm haunted nightly.
Because I'm made of grass,
I must move surely, lightly.

Because I'm made of feathers,
I must not fear to fall.
Because I'm made of fear,
you must come when I call.

Because I'm made of memory,
I live in an endless forest.
Because of appetite and will,
I must be always polished.

Because I'm made of earth and ash,
I keep my head bowed down.
Because I'm made of hope,
I sew my wedding gown.

Because I'm made of piss and shit,
I must live by grace alone.
Because I'm made of wheat and chaff,
I bide between two stones.

Because I'm made of air,
I've had to learn to share.
Because I'm made of darkness,
I rely on others' prayers.

Because I'm made of off-cuts,
I must write my own story.
Because I'm made of light,
I will not ration my glory.

Tom Thumb Visits the Crichton Institution for Lunatics

23 FEBRUARY 1845

It's a fine afternoon, almost on the edge of spring, when General Tom Thumb draws up before Crichton Hall. His equipage, which wins the first applause of the day, consists of a miniature chariot drawn by Felabella ponies, the smallest in the world, attended by an elfin coachman.

The cold sun shines on the tips of the General's shoes, where they edge out beneath the cats' tongues of his spats. It picks out the brass of the ponies' bridles and the sheen on the chestnut buds. Each sticky bud, before it bursts, will be fatter than the General's fists are now.

For three years, P. T. Barnum has honed Thomas Stratton's talents for this tour. The little General, now seven, has mastered the singing of songs in character (a *Havana Exquisite, One of the B'hoys*) and the dancing of the polka and the hornpipe. In costume, he will posture for you as Napoleon Bonaparte or Frederick the Great.

He arrives at the Crichton newly anointed as the rage of London society, having received no less than two audiences with the young Queen. Moreover, he's charmed gifts from the English nobility—from Queen Dowager Adelaide, a dainty gold watch and chain, made expressly for his use; from his Grace, the Duke of Devonshire, a jewelled gold snuff box.

In the recreation room, sun slants onto the stage from high windows, as if this were a cruise ship, freighted with misery, open to the unhindered light of the sea. The little sea-legs jig and the large head tops one more sloping-shouldered costume. The crowd —eighty-nine patients in all—watches, as attentive as any the General has known. Meanwhile Superintendent Dr William Browne and his attendants watch the crowd; for this is an anthropological regime, thirsty for knowledge.

Writing of the event in his annual report, Dr Browne's tone betrays some satisfaction that his patients showed more perspicacity than the cream of London society—and no doubt the crowned heads of Europe—combined. For he discerned, "a sound tone of criticism and enquiry as to the nature and tendency of the exhibition. Some philosophical minds were desirous to determine what [Tom Thumb's] capacities were, and whether, notwithstanding his histrionic or imitative powers, they were still infantile and undeveloped, corresponding to his size rather than his age." Others were drawn to speculate about gymnastic feats, through which, "to all a new, anomalous and suggestive impression was conveyed."

To suggest "an impression" is indeed the order of all their days. For Dr Browne is master of a system in which, "incessant watchfulness [is] exercised to arrest and destroy in their birth the vicious practices and ridiculous eccentricities of the insane." It is, in short, a system which pays, "tribute to reason by imitating its deportment, although it may be impossible to recognise or obey its law." Put another way, Dr Browne is also in the business of "honing acts".

Eighteen years later, at the little General's society wedding in New York, to the similarly petite Miss Lavinia Warren, the showman, P. T. Barnum, will present the dignified and bearded groom with a metaphor (later catalogued) that all who applaud his act this February day might recognise:

"an elaborately wrought casket of tortoiseshell. Upon pressing a spring, a diminutive bird, clad in natural feathers, rises from within, and sings very deliciously. It shakes its brilliant plumage, and is so exceedingly life-like in all its motions, that the spectator might be pardoned for believing it to be a genuine bird."

Nightwatch, 1842

When night falls and all others
have resigned their trust, I walk
the galleries, the guardian,
the master of all that stalks
their fitful sleep. I inquire
into all complaints, gratify
all reasonable desires.
I compel those with angry
and turbulent passions
to follow healthier trains
of thought. I give due ballast
to the most frivolous claims—
become master of reason
when I've need to flatter
the restless and the noisy:
"What spikes your night are *pictures*,"
I tell them. One's convinced
that shadows cut her like knives,
another dreams she's beset
by gangs of wizards and thieves.
To those who sing or whistle
or laugh; or to one who struts
the long gallery and chants,
"Dirty slut, dirty slut, slut . . ."
I'll bring the required balm.
The somnambulist I'll lead
back to bed like a child;
while to her who cries for "Auld
Auntie Peggy", my soft step
nears like a loved one,
giving fresh hope and healing
to her troubled mind. No sound
soils the night that can't be traced
back to its primary source.
From their soliloquies, songs

and prayers, I chart the course
of that wayward black river
whose stream's one moment choked
by rock and, at the next, split
in shallows featureless as smoke.
In the solitude of midnight
I notate such fractured plots.
When day commands the gallery,
another will take my watch.

The Last Vision of Angus McKay

Angus McKay, Queen Victoria's piper, went insane "over study of music". He was admitted to the Crichton Royal from Bedlam in 1856 when he was 43 years old. "His most prominent delusion is that her majesty is his wife and that Prince Albert has defrauded him of his rights." (Crichton case notes)

Let it be noted (in copperplate), Angus McKay
is a gentleman to watch. The stoutest furniture
is firewood to him; a mattress, within a day,
he'll disembowel. He has been known
to drink his own urine; to spit, shriek, howl
and hoot like an owl:
                        though this last
                        does not appear
                        in his case notes from Bedlam—
                        "hooting and howling" in southern parts
                        being thought not
                        abnormal for a Scot.

Nevertheless, there is enough on his native ground
to amaze and perplex his keepers.

Fuck it! Angus McKay has done with them all.

He eases himself into the rivercold waters of the Nith
across which lies Kirkconnell Wood
and his freedom. At that moment
                        (to which the record is blind,
                        no body being found, never mind
                        testament forthcoming)
something catches his eye—a sudden flurry and a bird
with two necks intertwined; one black, the other—
bodiless—a shimmering Islay malt brown.

Angus McKay watches, mesmerised

as the cormorant lifts its white-cheeked head
till its brassy twin—the eel—lifting with it,
unwinds like a flailing clef and falls, bit by bit,
into perfect darkness.

This, thinks Angus McKay, is how
the bagpipe has devoured my life.

He lies on his back, drifting downstream,
shadowing the black bag of a bird through flanges of light,
past two gracefully disinterested swans. The eel rages still—

the cormorant's neck rising and falling
in a helpless hiccup. Up ahead, the bird will calm,
its neck settle again on its shoulders—

but there, the quicksand waits to welcome Angus McKay,
sipping him, limb by limb, into its dark and clammy hold.

That evening, owls will keen—in Gaelic—
from Kirkconnell Wood, where Angus McKay
perches, pale and dripping.

> Will a soul never find peace? he asks.
> Oh, where has my plump little lover gone—
> and what's become of that shit, Prince Albert?

Field Notes

I found a woman, squatting
by a peat fire in the centre
of a bare room. With the exception

of a piece of old bag worn
like a shawl she was quite naked
above the waist. The house itself

is near to tumbling in
around her—ruinous, wretched,
comfortless: both wind and rain

have free entrance. Nor can words
do justice to the filth, dirt,
confusion and so on

and so forth. Vermin, faeces,
ruinous smells—you've read it
all before: how she

cannot tell the day
or the hour or count the fingers
on her hands, how she understands

nothing of religious truth. She lives
it is said on a cat's piss
of milk, yet still

monthly calls the children
around her, holding up two
red fingers like a flag.

Her husband has no words
but is capable of a growl
whenever he feels threatened

or excited. His habits—
dirty also: gapes, slavers, squints etc.
Words fail. Will not wash

but would embrace fire.
In good weather, nothing better
than to be led into a paddock

behind the stockyard. Here
he rolls incessantly (it is said)
a large stone (it is said)

from one end of the enclosure
to the other, till his hand (always
the right) (it is said) bleeds.

These unfortunates only meet here
as parents of a girl, blind at birth,
who crouches by a window

endeavouring (it is said)
to seek out the fugitive light
as it enters a broken pane.

The Buoy-Tree

Lochans of rain gathered
in the hollows, the trees
were dripping and bare.

On one, a gull landed,
spreading its wings like an angel.
It must have been a sign—

for angels are signs if nothing else.
Soon other gulls flocked there
till the whole tree was frocked

with them. Their wings beat
the water gently from them,
touching each other as you might

brush your arm against another
in a dance. It's a wonder
you never saw it that day,

it was all there was really to see—
a tree that seemed to writhe
with light, like a buoy

on a featureless sea.
But what drew the birds there,
or set them back in flight,

is just one more thing at which
to wonder. I can only think
it was the rain that kept you away.

Tryst

Watercolour by I (or J) Bannerman (c. 1861)
"In three of the productions, representing spots and
transactions in the Highlands, and imbued with
the most brilliant and blazing colours, the story
told is merely stupid and Quixotic."

DR. BROWNE in *Mad Artists*.

The tree twists
like a brown flame
fresh from the earth,

its stubby branches
end in green whorls
like fists. They

grasp an anger
that rages around them—
the wind-whipped grasses,

the clutch of reeds,
sturdy as swans' necks,
ready to strike.

A young woman's climbed
to this fruitless tree, trailing
her long green gown.

She turns to the tree
her blood-red cheeks,
the impassive wound

that is her mouth: the whites
of her eyes are intent
as arrows or as seeds.

Indeed, how fierce
must this tortured tree be
before she'll look away,

one arm still held
across her long green gown—
as above

the impenetrable
cocoons of clouds
scud by?

Landfall

Untitled watercolour, Crichton Institution for Lunatics

One man stands on an outcrop of rock.
With a boathook in hand, he stares out to sea.
In the cove below, two more male figures
do likewise. They edge into the thin light
where, in the shingle, a rowing boat waits,
oars in place, to take them from the island.

But what's brought them to this grey island?—
towered over by an armpit of rock
in whose shadow they do nothing but wait
at the edge of a febrile, silent sea.
Its waves reach the shore as tricks of light
in play on the faces of the figures.

That last is guesswork, for the three figures
have turned their faces from the island
towards two ships anchored on a line of light.
By one man, a boat-rope's wound round rock:
there's nothing to stop them putting to sea,
other than whatever it is makes them wait.

Yet they remember when they could not wait,
when everywhere they looked they saw figures
desperate for home and sick of the sea.
They'd be the first to visit the island—
already they loved its unyielding rock,
the earthly way that it spurned the light.

[24]

But once they landed, they climbed towards light,
heaving up the cliff-face their own dead weight,
searching for water and eggs in the rocks.
They found the cold imprints of figures
in the grass—waves of it crossed the island:
Even here, each had thought, *we are all at sea.*

They are three impounded by a mute sea.
They are given form by a leaden light.
Whatever they've witnessed on this island,
its significance for them must wait
to be revealed. From two ships, three figures
in thick suits seem to be turning to rock.

On a grassy sea, the islanders wait.
Soon light will leave these three frozen figures;
each a prisoner in his own black dock.

Charcot, Master of Salpetrière, Delivers his 'Tuesday Lecture' at the Crichton

AUGUST 1879

Monsieur Charcot—the Napoleon
of Neurosis—appears, framed
in a pool of light, much as he does

in the painting by Brouillet,
a copy of which will one day
hang over Freud's famous couch.

The local physicians, sturdy
descendants of Enlightenment,
reserve judgement as the patient,

Augustine, Queen of Hysterics,
falls back into an assistant's
open arms. Her top's come loose—

her breastbone's a winter table
in the stuffy room. Charcot
conjures from her a semaphore

of praying, begging, mourning:
her hands part to receive ecstacies
of grace. Of course they're familiar

with the photographs—the stylised
seductress in the loose chemise
staring out at them like a star

of the silent screen. But here, unveiled,
each pose jerks into its neighbour
as she lives out a story no one

cares to hear. Monsieur Charcot
bounces on his toes, while flames pour
from his mouth and the room glints

with secret terrors. His accent's
so thick only Latinate words
surface—*obfuscation, inner-*

vation, obnubliation. The words
fracture into flakes of ash that fall
on Augustine's naked breast.

Someone in the shadows sniffs.
"Materiality, my arse—
where words fail, I'll never follow."

The Arch of Hysteria

Every day she watched
as her mother, the Spider, wove
from her patience the colours and the shapes
back into threadbare tapestries.

Where there was a grey sky
she placed the sun, her fingers
so nimble and quick, she seemed
to soothe light through the landscape.

She gave liquidity back to water, perfection
to the moulding of each breast. The staghounds
bared their teeth once more;
the hunter's eyes were lit with horror.

It was her pleasure to restore to the world
(web upon web of tangled threads)
its purest sense of self. So that
when her daughter holds up a mirror now

she does not feel her father,
the Deceiver, behind her, but always
her mother, the Spider, small and nesting
in the cool shadows or arching over her

her great legs like a bridge. No one
will make her look away from the mirror
or from the knowledge that when
her body—or another's—arches in hysteria

or in passion, it's as if a thread spools
from her belly and she is drawn gently skywards:
testament to the power that always lay
in her mother, the Spider's persuasive hands.

Questions of Judgement

The Crichton Home Farm Steading, 1891

Everything here has its proper place:
grain in the granary, cows in their stalls,
carts parked in the dark arcades.

There each can be judged: the weight of grain,
the yield of cows, the greased wheels'
turning. And how easily

such judgements are made. Take
the Ayrshire bull, standing now
in the shadowy yard, his back

straight, forehead broad, rump
"level and long from hooks to pin-bones"—
no arguing with any of that.

Or that it's the proper place
of the farm manager, in cloth cap
and waistcoat, to hold the fine head

at show height, as another, almost
his twin, stands proudly—fists on hips—
at his side. Meanwhile

in the fields beyond, the "pauper
lunatics" labour. They are judged
by simple needs: a plenitude of food,

fresh air and exercise. Each evening
heading home, the huge clock-face
confronts them like a new moon

binding them to the slow seasons
of growth. *God Grant Grace.*
At night each, like a beast in the stall

of an almost-endless byre, watches
shadows from the dying fire play
on the ceiling. Some graze then

on a world beyond measure. Others
recoil, wondering in spite of it all, when
and just where they will ever fit in.

Deirdre

Because she was Deirdre,
Deirdre was simply who she was
and the world was dark
as an apple cellar, each apple
rotten to the core. So who
could she turn to, cast
down the steps, all alone
in the darkness, her small hands
feeling their way along damp walls
as she moved between those boxes
and boxes of shrivelled, soft fruit? Still,
their sweetness called to her
and, in the middle of each, she found,
past the waste of broken flesh,
five seeds, counting them out
on her fingers. She sang to them
of apples on a summer day,
shining in sunlight. She stroked
the tiny back of each one,
as it sat like a dark little flame
on her fingertip. Then she patted
the seed into a scraping of earth
at her feet. And she prayed
the apple prayer which calls
for a commonwealth of apples
to be shared wherever
there is earth and sunlight.
And the multiples of seeds grew
till shoots became seedlings
and seedlings trees—trees
whose thirsty crowns thrust
through the darkness of the cellar

and opened into light. Borne up with them
and dancing now from crown to crown,
gathering apples in her skirt
was Deirdre—
Deirdre of the Apples.

The Wolf Man at Crichton Hall, 1914

"In my story what was explained by dreams?
Nothing as far as I can see." The Wolf Man,
quoted in *The Wolf Man Sixty Years After*—
Karin Obholzer, 1982

The window opens in winter
and I am a child once again,
drawn by shouts, as I was back then,

to look out on a Christmas tree,
new-felled on the estate and brought
to my own window-side, for me.

But there are no baubles this time,
no angel glittering on top.
Instead on the silent branches

of a chestnut tree stand seven
white wolves, their eyes the sole candles,
their tails the only tinsel.

Time stops with seven white wolves.
Though a couple adjust their paws
from one branch onto another,

their broad heads stay perfectly still,
staring into the room where I stand
frightened to break this privilege.

For years I saw my mother thus,
four-legged and caught in moonlight.
For a moment without language

our eyes locked. Shame, anger or fear—
I felt the power of seven
times seven white wolves to wish me

away. But I've not been woken
by that image in years. Now,
looking at their wedding picture,

at her body in its white sheath,
pliant and ready for his, I share
nothing but her joy. No matter—

the seven white wolves still return
to stand in cold moonlight, to meet
my questioning gaze. I'm told now

they are images, conjured
from seven calico nightshirts
hung on a line. But I ask you,

if these are calico nightshirts,
then where are the seven white wolves
that were there in their place? They pad

along the frozen paths, between
Rutherford and Carmont, between
Dudgeon and Monreith, in the dark

ellipses of the night. And, while
these white nightshirts bandage the breeze,
seven white wolves howl at the moon.

And no my mother did not howl.
And no my father did not howl.
This is not a dream about love,

but about a sister tree, torn
from the old estate. Soon this one
will be brought, bleeding, before me,

hung with ribbons of flesh; while wolves
scavenge between Ypres and the Somme,
between Paschendale and Verdun.

A Dream Before Battle

In the night before battle,
the men lie in rank upon rank
on their bunks, barely breathing.
They think of the perfection

of their mouths, the treasures
of their eyes, of all that is tender
and beautiful that the next day
may tear apart. (In other rooms,

women, in their thoughts, redouble
those perfections.) Occasionally
a foot will stray from one bunk to
another, dangling down or across

in the most natural way, as if
it were a question of restlessness—
the old desire to be unbounded.
A hand greets it then, stroking it

as you do a stray kitten,
with surprise or delight—or as if
it were your son's. They marvel
at the shape of it, the give of it;

they read the leaf-marked map
of its sole. Bolder still, another foot
is somehow brought to meet it—
sole to sole. Yet the contortion

seems not so, for they remember
in just such a way they marked
time with their fathers. Now,
in the darkness, they father

each other, clasping both feet
within a single pair of hands.
And they smile with a sense of wonder,
as you do at marvels that can only

be brought within the covers
of certain, very special books.

Service Patient, 1916

Even in the cold dark days,
when Criffel's no more
than a black outline—a crouched

and headless beast—he prefers
to sit out on the veranda, to be
without walls. In the November *New Moon*

he reads a report from Miss McLeod,
matron on the *St. Andrew*, a hospital ship
on the Rouen to Southampton run.

"There is nobody on earth," she writes,
"like the British Tommy.

> Never
> a growl
> or a grumble;
> a limb off
> is nothing.
> They are so glad
> so surprised
> to be alive.
> Dear, brave boys . . .
> nothing's
> too good for them.
> A delicate slip
> of a boy of nineteen
> in today's load
> going home
> to his mother
> with his right leg
> and right arm
> off. It's
> heartbreaking
> yet she may

           consider
           herself
           and him
           lucky."

He looks up.
           Red-flagged ships
push end to end up the River Nith
as far as they can go. No longer can they

hold back the maimed and the wounded
from the farms and the villages which call them.
Up the narrow roads or stumbling

over the furrowed fields, through the hedges
they cannot see, they come at him,
falling, then rising, from the furrows,

the trenches and the fruitless briars.
Their writing hands are bandaged stumps.
They wave them in the frosty air.

Dear Alice

Dear Alice, Thank you for your last letter
with all its glittering tales of wonder.
You made *my* Neverland sound almost dull.
True, I'm in a rut with Hook. We spool
out all that old patriarchal nonsense,
an endless workshop to locate a lens—
a looking glass!—to show us what we are,
why we fight on and on, yet show no scars.
And you? You'll need lifetimes to unravel
the myriad meanings of your marvels.
Wasn't it Freud who said dreams of falling
concerned the act of love? The image rings
such bells with Tinkerbell. (Hope you don't mind—
she seizes all my letters. Zealous, but kind
in her own way, she's at least a regular.)
She took her red pen and fairy ruler
across all that nibbling and tasting too—
she claims both you and the White Rabbit knew
what he'd lead you to. Me, I'm captain
of my own ship, absolved from time's stain,
though I'll never step ashore. The sun
sinks now over these soft green hills.
Muffled, I hear geese's meaningless calls.
Somewhere, I've missed out on love, dear Alice.
Wendy tells me I don't know how to kiss.

Inmates

In the shade of sycamore and ash,
we made our encampment
of snow white beds. Below us,
the last frail nipples
of mushrooms, clover
and dandelion heads. Across
the windy spaces, skeins of thistledown
rose, swirled, idled. We
were no more than a hedge, a hut
or a wall: the seeds brushed us
and passed on their way. September
saw swifts like black scimitars
curving through the air, veering
towards the next instant of flight.
And this month? A powdered web
of thinnest rain, layered skirts
of sycamore seeds, ready for the off.
Soon, there'll be nothing
to stop us; with the first chill
of winter, we too will take flight—
down or up—into earth or air.
But like the human shells that twist
and turn at Pompeii,
those iron bedsteads will be left
curled around our absence.

Nurses

They took off their uniforms—
after all, it was so hot, the seams so stiff—

and lay them on the grass
like semaphores. The sun

beat on their young breasts,
till their skin cracked and flaked

the way of wood on the prows
of old boats. (I could take you now

to two or three that have sunk in river mud
and lie there, useless and unloved.)

So they stood, like wood themselves,
facing autumn with fortitude

till all fruit had fallen from them
and children cut their names—

Megan, Danny and *Frank*—
deep into their bark.

Freud at the Crichton

HOME MOVIE, SEPTEMBER 1939

The invitation had come from one
of the younger exiles: "Head north,
if you can, however briefly.

The blandness of a schnitzel
wouldn't be out of place
on any menu here and there's work—

Lord there's a whole nation
waiting for the couch." All true
of course, but he'd felt

suddenly tired in the well of the hall
where, even behind wire mesh,
the chatter of the patients (incessant,

driven) had reminded him
of the *Kaffeehaus*—everyone bent
over frothy coffees, all of them lipping

Kraft-Ebbing, Kraft-Ebbing, Kraft-Ebbing.

So it is in the Crichton grounds
we see him, come to watch
Jumbo, the Pekinese, run the run

that looks like a no-legged dash.
Even in grainy black and white,
which tricks us all into a jaunty grace,

he is composed—his right arm
crooked to his waist, in the left
hand a trademark cigar, his wrist

as slender and knuckled as any
in Egon Schiele. His cancerous mouth
is a pencil thin shadow of pain.

Braver hund, Jumbo, braver hund.

Inside, slicks of sunlight had fallen
from high windows, taken him back
to his rooms in Berggasse; the irony

that, in emptiness, they were finally
filled with light. Himself, he sees
as an interruption to the light

that will fill his space so very soon.
Though swifts tailor the air
with momentary designs that read like joy,

for him, there is no room for any
but very ordinary happinesses—the cigar,
the dog, the arm of Martha, his wife.

Together, they wander the nations—
Chestnut, Sycamore, Lime and Birch.
It's an early autumn here. He shivers

and they both head back up the path.

The Gardeners

This morning, an ivory mist
from which a few ragged trees
have stepped. Nothing else
and nothing screened from us.
The turbulence of the world's none other
than the singular will of a river
meeting the contagion of the sea.
                    Thus we know
how the Powers have risen
and fallen, no more than flowers
scattered through these evergreen woods.
Did they wish for well or for what
their opponents cried evil?
How differently did it feel
for those, however briefly, they bent
to their will? They saw themselves
as Gardeners too of course, faced
with overgrown ground.
We see it all as they did—
the choking weeds, the dead heads,
the lack of proper design. How else
to change it for the better
than by ripping, chopping, by a fresh set
of rules? *For good or ill*
our hopes must plan
beyond circumstance, as suffering extends
back, beyond its revelation,
in the contrary direction to hope.
These are only seeming things we sense
beyond the mist that encloses us.
But when we put our ears
to the cold ground, I tell you
somewhere near we hear another

brief experiment meet
its bloody end—
                        or it could simply be
cows in a nearby field, ripping
the grass up by its roots.

Grass

1. THE WEAVER

Is it true there's a man who makes clothes
out of grass? Yes, if it's long enough he makes
clothes out of grass. Where can you find them,
these garments of grass? Look beneath the holly hedge,
below the skirts of rhododendron. He takes little care
to hide them. So who are they for—these boots,
this jacket and vest, woven in grass?
They are for the weaver's own joy and to praise
the industry of hands. (They are also
for whichever of God's creatures
may find a use for them—mice
and small birds come readily to mind.)

2. THE ICEMAN

Of course there were those who told him,
      before he took off for the mountain pass,
that to survive all the snow and the jagged ice
      he'd need more covering than grass.

But he simply dons his coat of grass
      and his conical grass hat. Can't you see him
like something from a fair? *Man Made of Grass.*
      Then—even more the scarecrow—

he bends to his skin boots and crushes in
      as much as he can of (you guessed!) more grass.
A-ha, so he knows about skins? They all do—
      he and those who look on him now, lost

in amazement. They're draped in furs—
      the silver fur of a fox, the dark roast of a bear,
the fleeces of flocks fed on the rich grass
      that grows in the valley, before the forest masses

on the slopes where the hunters find their purpose
      and their songs. Their hearts come alive
with the blood-world around them. Grass
      has no god: this man is tinged with madness.

So when they see him leave the valley floor,
      they wave him off and feel their future blessed
with the power of the beasts they shoulder.
      There goes a sad man, they say, helpless as grass.

He never tells them that he carries his heart
        caught in a fork between high branches,
a blue sky above it; that it rests in its own nest of grass.
        He froze to death of course: nobody's loss.

Thousands of years later, an 'Iceman' is found,
        perfectly preserved on a mountain pass.
On a stone ledge beside him, plaited from grass,
        lies a rope, coiled like a noose.

3. RASHIN-COATIE

Let's interrupt the story, take time out.
Soon she'll go to the palace to seek work.

Soon she'll meet the prince and sure as day
marry him. She's living with the red calf for now—

the favourite she refused to kill, the one
who bore her away, naked, on his back.

Click-a-clack, click-a-clack, click-a-clack—
legs round your belly, rump on your back.

The calf's long pink tongue's latched
round some rushes by a loch. From them

she's woven a coat of sorts. Each day
the same palace guards laugh in her face

as they turn her away. Each night
she remembers her father dwelling

on her worthlessness, recalls
her sister's head falling in the sack.

Click-a-clack, click-a-clack, click-a-clack —
why would I ever ever want to go back?

Easier to thole, the years with the old bull,
his hot breath, his royally indifferent eye.

This then is her life, an interrupted story—
every day her hands held out,

her coat, long brittle, revealing
the remorseless narrative beneath.

Ex-Laundry Girl, 1943

If ever I'd the chance to choose my place
I worked the drying green. I eased off

my boots, let my feet grow sweetly cold
on the grass. We laid out the sheets

till they sat on the air like ruffled snow.
I smelled the sharp spoor of joy

a child leaves across a vacant field —
and wept a little for my loss. I wanted then

to be back inside, stoking that fire
till flat irons glowed like spearheads.

I wanted to be an angel of the damp air,
as smooth and shadowless as any sheet.

Something of that fierce heat fused the wires
in my brain. In church now when I sing

of 'hobgoblins' and 'foul fiends', I see them
in the finishing room, their eyes ringed

with sweat, yet no more fearful than the girls
I worked with. I've never shied since

from what is or whatever's to come.
So when the letter came about Jimmy

and the 'plane he was in, I wasn't numb
thinking of the flames that drowned him. Instead

I saw us rooted in a place we both knew—
one where you could stand talking with friends

as the flames licked round you again and again.
Again and again, again and again—

the flames lick round you again and again.

The Ghost Pitch

This morning, freezing mist's
screened the hills from view and though

a line of birch airily twist
against the white-grey sky, there's little

in them that could hold him back
or enfold him, the way the banking holds

that ghost pitch in its grasp, holds the slack
inflation of the pitch itself, a shaved

white cloud. This limited otherworld,
firm enough for a frozen-footed Jesus,

its few frosted chestnuts like giant pearls,
pulls him down to trace, beneath grass alert

with ice-spicules, the lines of the pitch—
a memory of summer. But not one

of those when the tines of each twig (rich,
green and endlessly flowering) draw

an easy kind of praise; or landscape
opens itself so generously, mountain,

river, ruin, match your reading of the map.
Rather when, head down, you launch yourself

into water or grass and for that moment
memory fails you: there is only

chill or salt or sweetness—the element
becomes you. So before this ghost pitch

there's no barrier. A tired explorer
with no future falls for a cold embrace,

his breath before him, a final prayer—

resistances

female admissions
1839

Resistances

each duty commands its own song
this gives it roots in the instant

while I polish while I sew
I give growth to what I do

～

you can hide under the eaves of song

in the same way
the heart of a spring crocus
beats secretly in its green sheath

～

laughter too lends a generous shade
it will be received unquestioned   rootless as the wind

～

I am indifferent to objects   unless
I can act upon them   in stealing
a pair of scissors   in concealing
a silver brooch   I find something
of what I am
                  a thin ravaged edge
it is this
which I do not wish to return

～

it is not important that you
find me   I dance

from one end of the room to the other
I circle myself
till exhaustion claims me

∾

I recast radiance
like a May tree in bloom

2.

because you dig the garden
it doesn't mean
you don't think the sky will fall in

it's only a position like any other

your foot on the fork
its tines smoothing through the earth

~

look at the dark horizon
or wait for the horizon to darken

~

who are my enemies

they have been as an army
will wash over the land

and leave some still digging

the fields red with blood
the turnips good

~

I have found a little shade
beyond here the world burns

you are best to keep silent
no one likes to hear bad news

~

there is nowhere to move on to
from here   no   I will not pretend
anymore   nor let you

3.

home has lost our touch
and so is lost to us

these annual visits
do nothing

but prove the distance travelled
is too great

～

the dressing table   the cooking spoon
the light slanting through the window

we are not where they are   nor do we
see ourselves in them

～

the world too has lost our touch
so we are the least deceived
the most free to act   where we

see flames we will say so
where the world drowns we will not avoid it

～

our own bodies leave us

~

from secret hidey-holes we watch
them hopelessly embracing
their own exile

4.

I watch

while the world punishes itself   it gives up
birds to fall from its sky   blossoms

to be torn from its trees   love
that it may be humiliated

~

the seas rage but they give up
                    their dead all the same
forests eat light to live on in darkness

~

a tide will dash the limbs
from a crab and still the crab live on

waiting for a gull to find it

~

I lose no more

than the world loses daily   the tide
is drawing from it and I am left

a crab spitting on the foreshore

～

understand this   my only hope
was to become stone

5.

how many steps in any direction
are to be trusted   the answer is three

~

beyond these three

there is an infinite number
of dangers which could befall you

nor beyond three steps
can you trust to your own innocence

~

for both these reasons you take
three steps with a constant mourning

as if you were a tree
with a wind weaving through its branches

~

it is well to know the world
over which you have command

a core where you can stand and say
what happens here is all I know

~

stamp out all other dreams

∼

I will let into my world
three things   air   light

and the trapped sparrow
matron took a brush to

6.

you make a bargain with the world
you say   I am not worthy of being on the earth

the world says   *work*

sew polish clean   read widely but wisely

⁓

you make a confession to your husband
you say   there are times when I wish you dead

he says   *work*

sew polish clean   read widely but wisely

⁓

in each activity you bless this house
but not yourself in it   the river

waits if only you could escape

⁓

a stranger saves you   you sit
on the riverbank to gather your breath

small birds dance on the sandbank
and watch the sea tide coming in

~

you want only one thing

that the world would efface you

7.

to remain yourself   deny yourself

~

the world recognises a fire
by its flames   rather

think of yourself as a calm sea
that cannot be mapped   no one

will wish it harm   few will care
what happens under its surface

~

the trick is not to care yourself   to live
truly in the negative spaces

she does not even   she neither seeks nor —
she never calls upon

~

the world moves with you
in this denial of light   as night falls

allow yourself the murmur
of a prayer   it is your duty to silence

that ensures you will be heard

~

over the frosted bulbs of the earth

ruins   brevity   dust

8.

lost soul there is a world
to be part of   all it takes is time

~

the accretions you have taken
to be your life did not reach

their ripeness in a day   how can you
hope to shed them in so short a time

~

if you embrace your exile
you will surprise yourself at what

can be so quickly lost   flesh
anger   memory   the storehouses

that flamed your life   you have bartered
their contents for this tranquillity

~

destitute of volition   free as a sea plant
you float with the disinterested tide

~

hold back only a small
mournful cry for the night and determine
that by your shit at least
they will know you

CODA

speak for me in a small voice
something indistinct that you might hear

on a forest walk but deep
in the darkness off the track   don't

~

speak with understanding   if you do
you've misunderstood what I am

~

look at the moon through the branches

there is almost music as the clouds
cover it   then let it go

~

that is not the moon I'm looking at

~

neither are you
the one to speak for me   not even daring

to raise your voice in the darkness

~

I could tell you things   oh
the things I could tell you   but again

you would sift them through the grid
of your understanding and then

you would not be speaking for me

～

which is all I ask
this clouded evening   that somewhere

in the silence   there is someone
who speaks   with indifference

in a small voice
for me

The Great Asylums of Scotland

The great asylums of Scotland, cloistered
like the proud abbeys we tore down brick
by brick. Yet harder to love. They docked
at the edge of our towns like relations
with whom we felt ill at ease. Ones who kept
themselves to themselves. Their farms. Their laundries.

Their water supplies. We stand in their portals,
our eyes drawn down the tree-lined avenues
to the prospect of distant hills. Country houses?
Hydros? Oh, what shall we do with them?—
the great asylums of Scotland, still with us,
as keen to serve as the day they were built.

A fleet for their time they set out, freighted
with hope and grand design. Look at them now,
scuttled on the ocean floor. Light floods them.
Along their corridors, doors flap open
on empty cabins with nothing to hide.
In attic rooms the sky's light pours over

a tide-wrack of maps, plans, records—a grid
to lay over a waste of rage, grief, anger
and pain. None of that will make a cairn.
In these, the great asylums of Scotland,
always it is evening about to fall.
The heavy doors are closing on us all

and the counting begins. But coming through
the frayed web of darkness are slants of light:
greenness, firstness, hope. What is to be done
with a two-faced legacy such as this?
Multi-occupancy—that's the answer!
Flatpacks to the gentlemen's quarters,

IKEA to the boardrooms. Four by fours
draw up before the great asylums now.
They're made for them, framed by chestnut trees,
like adverts. Inside the auction hall—
the stillness of graveyards, the discretion
of private affairs. Oh how beautiful

are the crafted dovetails in the wardrobes
no one wants. They sulk like small monuments
history has ignored. So much gloom.
'I wouldn't want any of it in my house,'
someone says. 'Not knowing where it's come from.'
As if objects soak up instability

like nicotine. If so, not only so—
for writhing up the staircase in Crichton Hall
are oak leaves, carved not by craftsmen from Antwerp,
but by men traipsing over winter fields
from Dalton using a water pipe as guide.
Run your hands over the leaves and you'll feel

their approval for their new asylum.
Though of the mad, little could be salvaged—
not one knitted pullover, not one apron—
for these craftsmen, the trade in lunacy
was a godsend. The melancholy we mourn
they transformed into bread, milk, sunlight.

Notes

SONG FOR M

The patient in question was admitted in 1839. "... during menstruation she plunged up to the middle in a pond to save a favourite hen which was in danger of being drowned." To my knowledge she was never released from care. I am grateful to Mary Smith for alerting me to her story.

FIELD NOTES

This poem draws on the Report of the Royal Lunacy Commissioners of Scotland, 1856.

FROM FOUCAULT

The two *Tales* are from anecdotes told in *Madness and Civilisation* by Michel Foucault, though I have changed the geography of the second from the Highlands of Scotland to the South West. The *Bedlam Ballad* is from the same source. Foucault tells of a man who thinks he is made of glass. In all other respects, his logic is faultless.

TOM THUMB VISITS THE CRICHTON INSTITUTION FOR LUNATICS: 23 FEBRUARY 1845

Drawn from the *Crichton Annual Report* of 1845 by Dr Browne and from *Sketch of the Life, Personal Appearance, Character and Manners of Charles S. Stratton, The Man in Miniature, Known as General Tom Thumb, And His Wife, Lavinia Warren Stratton; Including the History of Their Courtship And Marriage, with Some Account of Remarkable Dwarfs, Giants, and Other Human Phenomena, Of Ancient and Modern Times, And Songs Given at Their Public Levees* (Published 1863).

NIGHT WATCH

Patients were constantly watched for any untoward behaviour. At night their smallest cries were documented. This poem draws on the 'NIGHTLY STATISTICS OF NOISY PATIENTS FOR THE MONTH OF OCTOBER, 1842'. Freud, in his *Fragment of an Analysis of a Case of Hysteria* — or the Dora case (1905), compared "the hysterical narrative" to "an unnavigable river whose stream is at one moment choked by masses of rock and at another divided and lost among shallows and sandbanks."

Dr. W. A. F. Browne, author of 'What Asylums Were, Are, and Ought To Be', was the first Physician Superintendent at the Crichton Royal (1838–1857). While there he became one of the first collectors of Mad Art — what came to be known as Outsider Art, Art Extraordinary or Brut Art. These poems are based on two works from the Crichton collection.

CHARCOT, MASTER OF SALPETRIÈRE, DELIVERS HIS 'TUESDAY LECTURE' AT THE CRICHTON, AUGUST 1879

Jean-Martin Charcot was master of Salpetrière, the female asylum in Paris — "the great emporium of human misery", as he referred to it. There he photographed the female inmates identified as hysterics. Women enacted their particular type of hysteria before crowds at his 'Tuesday lectures'. Augustine became of one his most famous hysterics.

THE ARCH OF HYSTERIA

Takes its name from a work by sculptor Louise Bourgeois (b. 1911). It also draws on her biography.

THE WOLF MAN AT CRICHTON HALL

One of Freud's most famous cases. The Wolf Man had been a Russian aristocrat who had a recurring dream of seven white wolves in a walnut tree. Freud made a connection between this tree and the Christmas tree that was brought before his analysand as a child. Eventually (the analysis lasted four years), he traced the neurosis back to a "primal scene" when as a child the Wolf Man had caught his parents in the act of intercourse *a tergo*. Freud wrote the bulk of *From the History of an Infantile Neurosis* in autumn 1914, though it wasn't published till 1918. Rutherford, Carmont, Dudgeon and Monreith were four of the buildings on the estate of the asylum.

SERVICE PATIENT, 1916

The Crichton was in use during both world wars as a hospital and place of convalescence. The ships of the wounded echo the Ships of Fools Foucault describes, in *Madness and Civilisation*, adrift in the fourteenth century.

INMATES

This poem grew from *A Question of Taste*, a sculptural installation in
the Crichton grounds by Jan Hogarth in 2000.

FREUD AT THE CRICHTON

Because of Nazi persecution, several psychiatrists from Austria came
to work at the Crichton. Kraft-Ebbing was a sexologist in Vienna at
the turn of the nineteenth century. He wrote extensively about
sexual deviance. In a letter to Albrecht Schaeffer, dated 19th
September 1939, Freud wrote, ". . . I am more than eighty-three years
old, thus actually overdue, and there is really nothing left for me
but to follow your poem's advice: Wait, wait."

GRASS

Angus McPhee was a patient at Montrose Asylum in the 1970s–90s.
He made clothes and shoes and many other objects from grass. I'm
indebted to Joyce Laing's essay in Inner Necessity (ed, Pat Fisher) for
making the connection between Angus McPhee's work, the tradi-
tional tale of Rashin-Coatie and the grass clothes of the iceman.

RESISTANCES

This series is based on individual patient case notes. The patients
were all women admitted in 1839. I am grateful to Mary Smith for
providing me with painstaking transcriptions of these.

Don Quixote

"Today he's the unhappiest creature
in the world, the poorest too, and
tomorrow he'll have two or three
kingdoms to hand over to his squire."
(Don Quixote by Miguel Cervantes)

For whatever reason, it's common
that, after years of obstinate madness,
the mind recomposes itself. Women,
whose very names once gave the soul purpose,

become mired in time with the rest of us.
In this brief breathing space before the end,
our lives' adventures seem ridiculous:
the losses they brought too late to amend.

But still it falls to poor Don Quixote
to put right to himself and his companion
the wild falsehoods he mistook for glory.

"Don't die," Sancho pleads with the failing don.
Now he would exchange, for one last story,
three kingdoms on which the sun never shone.